God's Work

By Abe Usera

authorHOUSE®

AuthorHouse™
1663 Liberty Drive
Bloomington, IN 47403
www.authorhouse.com
Phone: 1-800-839-8640

First published by AuthorHouse 5/11/2010

ISBN: 978-1-4520-1036-6 (e)
ISBN: 978-1-4520-1035-9 (sc)
ISBN: 978-1-4520-1037-3 (hc)

Library of Congress Control Number: 2010904753

Printed in the United States of America
Bloomington, Indiana

This book is printed on acid-free paper.

This is dedicated to all that believe
In God and His work on earth
and
Especially my family

Acknowledgments

I would like to acknowledge a special thanks of gratitude to my dear wife Pat for helping me with the proof reading of my manuscript, and especially for being patient with me for the long hours and weeks while I was preparing my book.

Due to my computer not functioning to do what was needed to get things done for my book, I also want to thank my brother Deacon Luis A. Usera Sr. for assistance with helping me to get my materials prepared with the use of his computer for the production of my book.

INDEX

About the Author 1

Picture of Abe & Bishop 5

Picture of JFK Award 6

Introduction by Abraham Usera 9

Illustration of God's Work 11

Event #1 13

Event #2 17

Event #3 21

Event #4 25

Picture of Abe and Pat as Teenagers 28

Event #5 31

Event #6 35

Event #7 39

Event #8 43

Picture of Unborn Project 45

Event #9 47

Event #10 51

Event #11 55

Picture of Chief Abe Usera 57

Picture of 25th Renewal of Vows 58

Event #12 61

Picture of Abe as a Key West Police Officer 64

Conclusion of Events 67

Event #13 69

Picture of Christopher as an Altar Boy 71

Picture of Altare Dei Medal Presentation 72

Event #14 75

Picture of Antoinette as a Child 77

Event #15 79

Picture of Charity Work with Pat Usera 82

Picture of Police Cadets Graduation 83

Ending of the Events 84
Letter from Msgr. Michael Woster 85
Picture of God's Work – feeding the poor 86
Picture of God's Work – toys for the needed.......................87
Picture of Abe and Pat at St. Ambrose Church....................88
Abe's Family as of This Date and Time 2010........................89
Community Involvement..91
Recognitions..94
Letters of Appreciation from Organizations 97
Final Note..98
Closing Facts About Law Enforcement 99
Officer's in United States of America.................................100
Picture of Abe and His Family as a Baltimore City Maryland,
Police Officer. 101

About the Author

About the Author: Abraham Usera, known as Abe, was born in a building on Broadway, in New York City, New York, on November 22, 1944, to the parents of Beatrice and Libertad Usera. He had graduated from Franklin K. Lane High School, in Brooklyn, New York. Associates of Arts Degree in Criminal Justice Studies from the University of South Dakota, a Bachelor of Arts with Honors, in Criminology from the Saint Leo Catholic University, Saint Leo, Florida. He had attended many specialized Training Courses involving subjects pertaining to his Law Enforcement Career.

Abe had obtained some nick names during his life. When he was a teenager, he would wear his baseball cap backwards and also wore a French style cap. His friends would call him "Frenchie". One day in the summer of 1969, while working as a Police Officer for the Rapid City, South Dakota Police Department, he obtained his new nick name. Abe was patrolling the west side of Rapid City, when his Captain wanted to meet with him. He met his Captain name Roger at the Fitzgerald Stadium where the Shrine Circus was set up. Captain Roger said to Abe, if he would ride one of the Camels in the Circus, he would buy Abe breakfast. Abe took on the challenge and rode a Camel around the stadium field. That's when Captain Roger yelled up to Abe and called him "You Camel Rider". In the year of 1974, Abe attended the Baltimore City, Maryland Police Department, Police Academy. When attending the Academy some of the Rookies obtained nick names. Because Abe had a dark mustache and dark hair on his head which made him look like a Mexican, they gave him the nick name of "Friedo Bandito"

Abe has 10 brothers and 1 sister. His two oldest brothers William and Liberty were from his father's first relationship. The other 8 brothers and 1 sister are from Abe's mother Beatrice. They are John, Luis, Roland, Libby, Carlos, Julio, Isaac, Mario and his sister Carmen.

He was baptized on February 18, 1945, at the Our Lady of Esperanza Roman Catholic Church, in New York City, New York. As a small child, his parents along with Carmen, John and Luis moved to New Orleans, Louisiana. There his father worked as a Professional Musician, playing drums. His family lived there for approximately 10 years.

When Abe was a child in New Orleans he would volunteer to help the nuns at the church of Saint Alphonsus, by watering their garden and help cut the grass. He made his First Holy Communion at Saint Alphonsus Church on April 20, 1952.

At the age of 10 years old, his family now including Roland, Libby and Carlos, whom were born in New Orleans, moved back to New York City. When in New York City, Abe attended the Ascension Catholic School in Manhattan. There he served as an Altar Boy and was a member of the school choir. He made his Confirmation on October 28, 1955. While living in Manhattan, he would continue to do what God wants us all to do, and that is to help those in needs. So when ever he saw the Nuns carrying groceries, he would run up to them to help. He would carry their groceries to their home, which is a building next to the Ascension School. Abe lived on the same block, in a 2 room apartment with his one sister, eight brothers and mother and father.

In 1957, his father found a two family house in Brooklyn that had 4 bedrooms for rent. So the family moved there. He then attended Halsey Jr. High School for three years. He would volunteer to serve as a School Monitor and a School Crossing Guard. In 1959, Abe was given a Commendation for his volunteer work from his school Principal, a Mr. Joseph Gordon. At the age of 13 years old Abe would serve as an Altar Boy for the Fourteen Holy Martyrs Church, in Brooklyn. When he reached the age of 14, Father Mahoney at the Fourteen Holy Martyrs Church requested Abe to help with the boy's basketball team, as being their coach. While living on Halsey Street in Brooklyn he would be the protector for his 6 younger brothers and sister from the near by gangs. His older brothers were involved with their friends at the old neighborhood in Manhattan and other activities not in Brooklyn.

At the age of 18 going on 19, he married his best friend since age 14, Patricia Ann known as Pat. There were people out there at that time didn't think it would work because of their ages and race. Abe is Hispanic and Pat is of Italian descent. So they got married by a Justice of the Peace in Brooklyn on the 18th of October 1963. Pat and Abe felt something was missing in their lives. They felt they needed to get married in the Catholic Church. So they got married again at the Saint Martins of

Tour Catholic Church in Brooklyn. As of this date and time of the year 2009, since they met, they have been together for approximately 50 years. They were blessed to have two children, Antoinette and Christopher.

Due to the riots and crime in 1968, Abe moved with his wife and children to South Dakota for a better environment for his family. While living in South Dakota Abe and Pat had lost a child at birth in 1969 and their 21 year old son Christopher in an accident in 1987. They both have 5 grandchildren. Antoinette has 4 boys and their names are Jesse, Keith, Alan and Jeremy. Christopher had a girl born after his death by the name of Amber. Abe had a career in Law Enforcement and Pats career was in the Medical Field. He also held positions in Law Enforcement in the City of Baltimore Maryland, and The City of Key West, Florida.

Wherever Abe lived, he always continued to do God's Work. Some work consisted of volunteer activities. He was also recognized by many various professional people and organizations for his work. He had never asked for any recognition and always felt it was his duty under God to do the right thing by helping those in need of help. It was truly his faith that helps guide him to be a better person in life. He was involved in many events that made him a Hero and he never took them for granted.

Here are some of the following volunteer work and recognitions involving Abe: Served as the Grand Knight for the Our Lady of the Perpetual Help Council 1489, in Rapid City, South Dakota. He was chosen as the JFK Knights of Columbus, Knight of The Year 2000, for the State of South Dakota. He held the position as Internal Director for the Rapid City Jaycees. He was chosen as the 1977 Outstanding Young Man for his community work and also the 1980 Outstanding Young Law Enforcement Officer. He had also volunteered to serve as a United Way Chairperson, Cystic Fibrosis Chairman, International Sports Board member, Indian and White Committee Board member, Child Abuse Team Board member, Alcohol / Drug Abuse Team Board member, all of Rapid City, South Dakota. Served on the Box Elder City, South Dakota, Equal Employment Opportunity Commission. He held the position as Scout Master for The Knights of Columbus Council 1489 Boys scout Troop 7. He was involved as Scout Master in producing 19 Eagle Scouts. It was the most Eagle Scouts any Scout Master had produced in the Black Hills Area Boy Scouts Council. For his Christian leadership in scouting, Abe was presented by the Western South Dakota Diocese, Bishop Harold Dimmerling; the Saint George Medal. He also served as the Advisor for the Rapid City Police department Explorer Post 110- Police Cadets. Also in Rapid City he managed several Harney Little League Baseball Teams. As an Instructor for the American Red Cross, he taught CPR and First Aid. Participated with the Special Olympics Torch Run in South Dakota and Key West Florida. All of the aforementioned organizations held many activities which consisted of many hours of volunteer work.

Abe and his wife Pat did a special volunteer work for the Mission of Saint Isaac Jogues Church in Rapid City. Father Patrick McCorkell, S.J., obtained an autographed football Jersey from the Denver Broncos to be used for a fund drive. So Abe and Pat put a raffle together to help raise money for the fund drive. Abe and Pat also went to several churches in the Western Diocese to sell raffle tickets. For a few weeks, they spent time after each mass on every Saturday and Sunday. The results of their hard work turn out to be the best single Fund Raising Project St. Isaac Jogues Church ever had. This was quoted in the letter written by Father Patrick McCorkell to Abe and Pat, dated January 15, 2002. You will now have an understanding how God worked with Abe.

Abe receiving the St. George Emblem for his services to the Catholic Scouting program and his years of Service to the Rapid City area Boy Scouting. Bishop Harold Dimmerling presented Abe the Emblem with Mayor Art LaCroix giving the welcome speech.

South Dakota JFK Knights of Columbus Knight of the Year 2000

Left to Right: Supreme Representative - Judge Richardo Garcia, Abraham Usera, Patricia Usera, State Deputy - Leo Keiser

South Dakota Knights of Columbus had in the year 2000, 8,000 members and 77 Councils

Introduction

INTRODUCTION
BY
ABRAHAM USERA

Throughout my life, I had gone through so many events. Some of the events involved some of the following: The lost of my 21 year son and unborn child. Throughout my childhood and adult life, I had to deal with racial prejudices. Especially the prejudice acts against me while working in my career as a Law Enforcement Officer. The many case investigations I was involved with as a Law Enforcement Officer. Also consist of growing up in a large family and medical problems. The music I wrote and sang. And the sporting positions I held. There were many good and some bad times of events in my life. But I feel it was God that got me through my ups and downs in life. I truly believe too much cannot be said about "God's Work" on this planet of earth.

The content of this book has accurate perception of what it is like to be a believer of God's Work. It consists of events that are heart-touching to all that understand and believe in God. The events are true to the best of my ability. I truly believe it was the help of God that got me through the events described in this book. Without the help from God, I would not have the strength and will to do the right thing at the time of each event. There are people out there that truly believe I am a Hero. It has been my belief; I did not take action to do the things in each described event on my own. I feel it was God's Work that got me through it all.

I also want you the reader to know there are many heroes out there that are involved and hope you will have an understanding what they all mean to us all. They consist of my Family, Law Enforcement Officers, Firefighters, Emergency Rescue Teams, Medical, and Military personnel. There are many everyday citizens out there that also get involved

When reading the enclosed events, you will observe they took place throughout my life. This book also talks about my wife, daughter and son's personal experience with "God's Work".

In the contents of the enclosed events, I have left out the names of the victims not related to me, to protect their privacy. You the reader might find that you had been in a similar situation in any of the enclosed events. Hopefully this book will get people to relate to any of the events and able to talk about God's Work.

Enjoy and God Bless

They found Mary and Joseph and the infant lying in the manger. Lk. 2, 15-20

THEY·ALL·ATE·AND·WERE· SATISFIED.   MT 14: 13-21

God's Work

A Sumaritan traveler who came upon him was moved with compassion.

Lk 10:25-37

I WAS BLIND AND NOW I SEE.
JN 9: 1 - 41

Event #1

EVENT #1

It was the year of 1952, when I was approximately eight year's old, living in New Orleans, Louisiana, when this event took place.

It was a warm and beautiful sunny day in New Orleans. My brothers John, Luis, Roland and my sister Carmen were playing in the back yard with other children from the neighborhood. Our neighbors were good people to us. One of them name Ms Price lived up stairs from our family. She would always bring to our family some Lemon Aid. As a small kid, I always thought she made the best Lemon Aid in the World. Maybe it was because of the egg shape and juicy fruit taste that I loved about the lemon. When ever Ms Price would buy a large bag of lemons she would always have some ready to give to me. It was a treat when she gave me the lemons.

My mother was inside the house and I was just sitting on the front porch enjoying my tasteful lemons, when there appeared to be a sound of loud music coming down the street. It was a sound of music familiar to all the kids in the neighborhood. It was the Traveling Merry Go Round Truck, which had small wooden horses on it. When the truck arrived near my house, it parked across the street from where I was sitting. The music would continue to play on. The children in the neighborhood all ran to their parents for money to get on the ride. You see the price for a ride on the Merry Go Round Truck at that time was five cents. I also pleaded to my mother for a nickel. She said she didn't have a nickel on her. Standing next to her was Ms Price. Ms Price said she had a nickel and offered it to me to go on the ride.

So with a happy face and with excitement, I proceeded to cross the street to get on the ride. All the kids including me were having a lot of fun laughing as we went round and round with the music playing. When most of us got off the Merry Go Round we were a little dizzy. As kids we kind of laughed about it. After the ride I started to cross the street, when suddenly things had changed my life. That's when a speeding car driven by a female drunken driver hit me.

As my mother recalled, she said I flew up in the air and landed on the street, a few feet from the vehicle. Moments later I recalled waking up seeing my mother looking down at me crying. I was also crying with a lot of pain. Within moments after that, I black out. The next time I can recall waking up and looking up at my mother and the ambulance personnel. At that time I was lying on the stretcher inside the ambulance. My mother was still crying and saying, "Oh my God don't let anything happen to my baby". "You will be alright Baby". The attendants also said to me "everything will be okay". That's when I black out again. On route to the hospital I can hear the sound of the sirens coming from the ambulance.

When I arrived at the hospital I woke up to see a man dress in white style uniform clothing. He had in his hands a large metal ice cream cone shape object. I learned later it was used to stretch my broken bones. The procedure hurt so bad I black out again. One of the most important events in my life then took place. I woke up again and observed a Catholic Priest given me my last Rites.

As he was blessing me I fell asleep. I found myself walking down a colorful path to a beautiful garden and play ground. Holding my hand was a Man dress in a white robe type garment with a beard, and dark shoulder length hair. There were many children playing and laughing without any pain or injuries. I also felt no pain at the time. The man looked down at me as we were walking and said in a pleasant voice, "It's time for you to go back home". Because of my teaching of my faith, I truly believe it was "Jesus Christ". This was a time in my life that I truly believe that it was God's Work that took place.

As I woke up again, I found my self in a hospital bed with my legs and arms in tractions. It was a happy moment for my mother and personnel present to see me wake up again. It was special to see me with a smile on my face. They were not aware of the trip I took to the beautiful garden and the man dress in white that gave me the smile of my life. I did not say anything to them because I felt they wouldn't believe me. It took several months to get better. I was sent home in a body shape cast. I needed to get help to eat and other personal hygiene matters. It took many days throughout a year with hard work and perseverance, to do the therapy to walk again. With many prayers and with the help of God's Work,

I got through it all. I grew up to play sports and enjoy my life to the fullest. You see it took many years in my life to talk about this special event. I always thought people would think I was crazy or just making it up. I than decided in the year 2000 to tell my story, after reading about people having after life experiences and their contacts with persons that appeared to be God,

No matter how people feel in their heart about our God, I will always believe in God's Work.

Event #2

EVENT #2

It was a cold day in winter in the year 1957. I was 12 years old, living in Manhattan with my family. The kids in the neighborhood would all play in the street or walk to Riverside Drive Park. Riverside Drive Park runs right next to the Hudson River. There many kids would enjoy fishing and sledding in the snow on near by hills. The other area the kids would walk to is Central park to enjoy sledding as they do at Riverside Drive Park. The kids on the block would go to the two parks because there wasn't much to do on the block that we lived on. Also at Central Park is a small lake. Many people would go ice skating on the lake when it was safe to do so. A couple of my friends on the block ask me if I wanted to go to Central Park to go sledding. Because there wasn't much to do on our block I advised them I would get permission from my mother. With the approval from my mother and their mothers, we proceeded to walk to Central Park.

While sledding on some hills in the park we observed some boys from another neighborhood crossing the icy lake. They were walking from the other side of the lake to a small Island in the lake. Understand the Island is not very large. It was approximately 50 feet from the area of land we were at. The kids that reached the Island then started to call us to join them. So my two friends, Billy and Steven and I decided to walk across the lake to the Island. We felt that if they made it with out any problems, we also shouldn't have any problems. So we started walking on the icy lake towards the Island. As we were approximately 10 feet on the ice, we heard some cracking sounds. It appeared to be coming from the lake.

We were 12 year old boys not really understanding what was about to happen. We did ask each other if we should keep walking to the Island and we all agreed to do so. The ice seemed to be solid in the area we were walking so we continued on. It wasn't too long after the first cracking sound, another one came about. I told my friends to stop and remember we have our Guardian Angels to protect us. Just moments after I said that the ice started to make a loud cracking sound. The ice broke right under our feet and we all fell into the frozen water of the lake. The area of the lake we fell into was approximately 8 feet in diameter. We desperately kept reaching the flat area of the lake next to where we were at. We started to cry because we thought it was the end of our lives. As I called out to God, to please help us, I was then able to dig my hands on to the flat area of the lake and pulled my self out first. Understand this incident didn't take long. I immediately laid flat on the ice and grabbed one of the boys first. We than pulled the other boy together out of the water when we both got out. We all lay back on the ice and looked up to the sky to thank God. We all got up and looked at each other shaking. Without any thought we all started to walk back to the main land. There was no way we were going to go to that Island where the other boys were at.

We proceeded home with our wet clothes on. When we arrived home we observed our clothes were almost completely frozen. The weather had gotten colder by the time we arrived home. We were all students at Ascension Catholic School. When we were in church together, we prayed to thank God for his help. Because of our faith we believe that was the right thing to do. I specially thank God for giving me the strength in helping my friends out of the water.

We learn later that the area of the lake we fell through was approximately 6 to 8 feet deep. My friends and I were approximately 4 feet tall.

This again was "Gods Work".

Event #3

EVENT #3

It was the year of 1957, when my family and I were living in a two room apartment, in the upper Westside of the Borough of Manhattan, New York City. My father advised my family, he had obtained a four bedroom house in Brooklyn for rent. So we all packed up our belongings to move from the predominantly Irish neighborhood to the borough of Brooklyn. Our family at the time consisted of my Father and Mother along with my sister Carmen, and brothers, John, Luis, Roland, Libby, Carlos, Julio, and my self. When we arrived at the dwelling in Brooklyn, we were all excited because there were more rooms for us to share. The house was located on Halsey Street located in a neighborhood of mostly Jewish and Italians. Our family was one of the first Hispanic Family to live in the neighborhood. The neighbors were very kind to us and offered my family any assistance if needed. I personally felt at the time the neighbors were very generous and kind, because they saw a large family that did not have the essentials for normal living.

When we lived in Manhattan there were gangs. Some of the gangs in Manhattan were called the Dragons, Baldies and Chaplains. We were lucky at the time when we lived in Manhattan, the gangs were not present in our neighborhood. But living in Brooklyn was another story. There were the Black, Hispanic and White gangs in Brooklyn. Some of the Black gangs were called the Mow Mow Chaplains, Stumpers, and Jefferson Street Stumpers. The Hispanic gangs that I can also recall were the Flaming Saints and the Spanish Ellery. The White gangs that were associated with my neighborhood were the Halsey Street Bops, the Ellery Bops and Railroad Boys. Other White gangs in Brooklyn were the Rockaway and Fulton, The Lords of Flatbush and the Canarsie Street Bops.

At 12 going on 13 years old I attended Public School, Halsey Jr. High School located in my neighborhood. The school consisted of many white and some black students. The Hispanic population at the school was very minimal. So you can understand why it was a little scary to attend a school not knowing the students at first. The church our family attended in our neighborhood was Fourteen Holy Martyrs Catholic

Church. There I was an Altar Boy for approximately two years. My two older brothers, John and Luis were attending Cardinal Hayes Catholic High School in the Bronx. They both would travel back to Manhattan to hang out with their friends. John at one time was at a Catholic Seminarian School for the study of the Priesthood. So you can understand why I was left to be the protector for my family. Throughout the time I lived on Halsey Street, I got to know most of the kids in the neighborhood. There were times the gangs would go into a battle stage. The wars between the gangs were mostly racial motivated, between the White and Black gangs.

As the protector for my six younger brothers and sister, it made me more want to count on God, with prayers to help me. There was a time when I observed a black boy walking home from Halsey Jr. High School through our neighborhood, when a few white boys had approached him. Because there was a war between the Halsey Street Bops and the Jefferson Stumpers, the Halsey Street Bops members wanted to hurt the black boy. The black boy was from the Jefferson Street Stumpers neighborhood. I approached the white gang members and pleaded to them not to hurt the black boy. They knew me because we live in the same neighborhood. I finally got them from hurting the small boy. The boy looked at me with tearing eyes of thankfulness and quickly left the area.

When I was approximately 14 years old, I was approached by Father Mahoney at the Fourteen Holy Martyrs Church. He requested my help to coach the boy's basketball team. I was also a player and captain on the team. Something came up that we had no one to take us to the game at Canarsie. Sports were one of my hobbies that kept me out of trouble and I agreed to help. So I gathered up the team members to travel to the Canarsie area of Brooklyn. We had to travel by the Subway trains to get there. It was a fun trip for all of us. We joked and laugh about things while on the train. It was also a beautiful day in the winter. The team didn't win our game, but enjoyed playing. We finished with a prayer and started to head home.

When walking to the Subway, we were approached by a black gang of boys. They demanded money and threaten to hurt us. I did not see any weapons on them and I felt they would use their fist to hurt us. That's when I said to my self, "please help me my Lord Jesus Christ". I quickly got in front of my team members and begged the gang not to hurt them. I confronted their leader to fight, while the boys headed towards the Subway Station. We got into a fist fight and some bystanders yield at the gang to leave me alone.

The gang was from another neighborhood, looking for trouble. I was left with a black eye and headed back to our neighborhood with the team members. The boys all appreciated my will to protect them from harm by hugging me and patting my back. I told them to thank God for our rescue. I did thank the few people that were in the area when I was trying to get away from the gang. When we arrived back from the game, I advised Father Mahoney of the incident. He said, thank God no one got serious hurt from the incident. I looked at Father and said, "What about my 'Black Eye'". We kind of laughed about it, but knew he appreciated my will to protect the team members from getting hurt.

You see without the help of our God things could have gotten worse. The people that were in the area that yelled at the gang members had in their hearts to help thy neighbor as thy self.

The good actions taken by all involved was truly of "God's Work".

Event #4

EVENT #4

As it was mentioned in the previous Event #3, I had the responsibility of being the leader and protector of my younger brothers and sister. My sister and I would at times help with the chores at our house and that included watching over our younger brothers. My sister is approximately eleven months older than I am. It was the year of 1960, when I met my best friend and Puppy love, as it was said in those days. It has to do with our ages as being teenagers. Her name is Patricia, known as Pat. That's when she also became a good friend and sister to my sister Carmen. It was also one month after my brother Mario was born, when Pat came into the picture. My brothers loved to have her around. They were fascinated with her beauty and compassion towards them. She would even go with me to church with my younger brothers. How many guys out there would actually say this has taking place in their lives? That means having a teenage girl friend, putting up with being around so many children. I can recall when I first brought Pat to our house, my younger brothers would all line up by the front window to see who I was with. They were not use to seeing any one of their older brother's girl friends at the house. It has always been part of our good memories in our lives.

One of the most important memories of that time is the event that takes place in this Story. It was in the summer of 1960, when the weather was a beautiful sunny day. As kids, we appreciated school was out for two months. My father was at work and my mother was doing her domestic chores as always. Pat and I were getting ready to go to Coney Island.

Coney Island is a famous Recreational Park with games, rides and a beach next to the Atlantic Ocean. Pat, a kind person as she was, suggested it would be a good idea to bring some of the boys with us to Coney Island. So I advised my mother we were willing to take some of the boys with us for a day at the beach. My sister decided to stay home with my mother to help with three of my younger brothers, Roland, Isaac and Mario age two months. Mother was very pleased to have us take my brothers Libby seven, Carlos six and Julio five years old. The money used to go to Coney Island was from my part time job. I worked at the Paradise Shoe store near Halsey Street and Broadway, Brooklyn, as a Shoe Salesman. So we all headed out to get on the Subway Train to travel to the southern part of Brooklyn, to Coney Island. The ride on the subway at that time was ten cents for a one way trip. In those days we were not afraid to ride the subways at our age, especially during the day time, because there were many people traveling at the same time.

When we arrived at Coney Island, we all ran to find a spot on the sandy beach, near the ocean water. The boys were so excited, while running to our spot they started to take off their clothing that was over their bathing suits. You see because of the large crowds, you have to get there early in the morning to claim a spot, especially if you wanted to get near the ocean waters. Pat and I laid out the blanket on the sandy beach area where we settled down. The boys immediately started playing with the sand, building sand houses. They also covered themselves with the sand. It was nice to see them having a good time. It was also funny to see them run into the water. Especially when a big wave would approach them, they would quickly run back on to the sandy beach. Everything was going well for Pat and I and the Boys. It was time for lunch. So I started preparing the sandwiches and Cool Aid for all of us. We would use the spot where our blanket laid, with our clothing and towels. Pat was with Carlos, getting him ready to get out of the water to join us at the blanket for lunch.

This is when the main part of this chapter of Event took place. A larger than most of the waves with a strong undertow, approached Carlos as he was leaving the ocean waters. The wave had enough power in it to pull Carlos further into the Ocean Waters. Pat immediately screamed over to me and she dove into the water trying to get to Carlos. She was unsuccessful reaching him, as the wave kept carrying Carlos out into the Ocean Waters. I immediately dove into the water and started to swim out to reach Carlos. As I was swimming towards Carlos, the ocean waters just kept pulling him in and out of the water, heading further out. As I was swimming to reach Carlos I kept calling out to God to please help me get my brother. "Oh God", please, please help me! It must have been approximately fifty yards from the sandy beach out in the ocean when I saw Carlos going down for the last time. He was approximately six to ten feet from me. I dove into the dark ocean water hoping I could reach his hands. As I dove into the water I was crying and thought it was the last time I would see my kid brother. Again I pleaded to God for his help. As Carlos was sinking into the dark waters a light appeared to shine around Carlos. I reached for his hand and pulled him up to the top of the water. I knew then, God's Work went into action. I held on to Carlos and swam back to shore.

When we got to shore Pat and the boys were very happy with tears in their eyes, to see that we made it back to the sandy beach area. Pat grabbed Carlos with hugs of love because she was happy to see he was alive and well. It was great to see Carlos breathing and crying with happiness to be back on land and with his brothers. The Life Guards were involved with other people in the water at the time this event took place. It happened so quickly, by the time they were able to get to Carlos it would had been too late. So we waited for things to cool down from the excitement to head home. We packed up our things and traveled back home on the Subway Train. When we got back home we told my mother about the incident involving Carlos. As a true believer in our Lord Jesus Christ, she said "Thank God you saved Carlos". I told my mom how I kept yelling out to God for his help. My mom said it was great God had listened to me.

Carlos as of this year 2009 had done good through out his life. He went on to be a good student in school. He attended West Point after graduating from high school, and retired as a Major for the United Stares Army. He is married to Maria and has three sons and one daughter. He and Maria are also grand parents. He is also a member of the Knights of Columbus.

This was truly "God's Work".

Abe and Pat Usera as teenagers in Brooklyn, N.Y.

Event #5

EVENT #5

It was the year of 1968, when the United States of America was going through some bad times. These times considered of the Vietnam War and the Black Riots through out the large Cities. At that time my brother Luis was serving in the United States Air Force. My brother John was in the Marines, and my brother Roland was in the Army. They all served in Viet Nam. The City of New York was going through hell with the racial riots. Many people got hurt and many property damages took place. There was a lot of fear to live there at that time. My brother John was getting out of the service and was heading back to South Dakota. There he would resume his job teaching, which he had before going into the service. At that time Pat and I had two children. Antoinette age four and Christopher age two. I had the opportunity in my life to live some where else besides New York City. Pat had always lived her life in Brooklyn. I felt it was time to find a better place for my family to live.

I contacted my brother John and explain to him about my concern for my wife and children to live in a better environment. He explained to me about South Dakota and its environment. After our conversation I felt it was time to make a move. I talked it out with my wife and with out any fuss she approved of the decision. So we packed up our belongings and headed out to South Dakota in a U Haul Truck and our 1957 Pontiac. It was a little scary for my family knowing we were all going to a strange place. My brother John helped with driving one of the vehicles to South Dakota.

When we arrived at the eastern part of South Dakota, the Sky was so clear with beautiful Powder Puff shape clouds. As we traveled heading west through the state, we couldn't believe how much land there was. Where we came from you were lucky to see fifteen feet of land next to the dwelling you lived at. When we arrived in Rapid City, South Dakota we didn't have any problems finding a house to live in. It was hard for me to believe that I could buy a three bedroom house with $200.00 down and $104.00 a month payments. Just to know my children had their own bedrooms and we had our own master bedroom was a great feeling things would get better for us. It was really nice to have good neighbors. At that time the City of Rapid had the Welcome Wagon for new residents. My brother John went back to the Pine Ridge Indian Reservation to resume his teaching Job.

My first Job was at the C & C Goodyear Tire Company at the corner of 4th Street and Main. The business consisted of tire sales and vehicle maintenance. The manager in charge was a Mr. Russ Haley. I can always say he was one of the best persons to work for. Within three months I was promoted to be the Warehouse Manager. There were five warehouses which included the Main store for my responsibility. An area of the store that involves this event is the Tire Service Department. There was a young man at the age of eighteen that was working on the day of the event. The store handled many tire sales that day which made it a very busy time for all of us employees. It all started when the young man had a small trailer tire to be replaced for a new one. So he went into the area in the store where the new small tires were located at. He found a tire to replace the old tire the customer brought in. He went back to the area where he worked on busting tires. He placed the old tire and wheel on the rack. He deflated the air from the old tire and removed the old tire off the wheel.

During that time, the rest of the employees and my self were doing our jobs away from the area where the young man was at. I was just outside the door that led into the area where the young man was working. A Semi Truck was backing up to the big doors that led into the store tire storage area. As warehouse manager, I was there to help unload the new tires off the Semi Truck. I also had to inventory the shipment. During that time, the young man was placing the new tire on the wheel. He began to inflate the new tire, using the Air Compressor. That's when the tire blew up causing a loud explosion sound. I was just outside the door where he was at, when the incident took place. It appeared the tire blew up in pieces and also causing the rim to blow off the tire and wheel rack. I immediately ran into the store to the area where the young man was working. I can hear some of the employees in the store yelling out for some one to call for an ambulance. As I approached the young man I observed he was bleeding on his arms. He was on the ground, lying face up. His face was very blue and discolored. I check to see if he was breathing and observed no breath from his mouth. So I started to do CPR, mouth to mouth breathing on the victim. Another employee came over to assist me with the CPR, was the Wholesales Manager, name Tom Douglas. The victim also had received injuries to his chest. The injuries were caused by the rubber from the tire. And also the wheel blew off the rack onto the victim's body. As we were continuing CPR, the Ambulance arrived. The ambulance attendants took over the medical help for the victim. He was then transported to the Rapid City Regional Hospital for medical treatment. As he left the store in the ambulance, my fellow employees and customers thank Tom and me for our actions to help save the young man's life.

All I could say at that time was, thank God he will be alright. Weeks later the young man got better. He met up with me and gave me a big hug with tears and joy of thanks. He said, thanks for saving his life. As always, I responded by saying to him, thank God for giving you life. After an investigation of the incident, it appeared the new tire was a wheel barrow tire instead of a trailer tire. The tires were the same size. The air pressure in a wheel barrow tire is not the same as a trailer tire. So by placing too much air in the wheel barrow tire had caused the tire to explode.

The Young Man as of this year 2009 is in his fifties. He has a family and works as a Painter in Rapid City, South Dakota. When ever he sees me, he always thanks me for his life. I always tell him to thank God.

This was indeed "God's Work".

Event #6

EVENT #6

It was the summer of 1972 my family and I were living in Rapid City South Dakota. The day was June 9, and it was a cloudy and rainy day. It appeared we were getting more than usual rain that day. As I was listening to the radio while in my vehicle, I heard the radio announcer say the rain is causing flooding in the Black Hills and for people to seek higher ground. He also said the flood waters will hit the Rapid City area. I observed my house was getting lot of rain water pouring into our basement. I thought I should warn the people in the Canyon area west of the Canyon Lake Park to clear out from the area because of the warning of flooding. My good friend Don and his family lived in the Canyon area at the time. After the flood waters hit the Black Hills and Rapid City, many homes and businesses were damaged. There were many deaths that also took place. The city of Rapid City was devastated due to the results of the flood. The Mayor declared Martial Law. I felt it would be a good time to send my wife and two children back to the east coast to spend some time with my wife's family. So they went by Greyhound Bus to travel to New York City. I stayed back in Rapid City to help those in need.

After everything cool down for a while, I then drove my vehicle to the east coast to pick up my wife and two children. When in New York, my mother in-law, Helen, my sister in-law Geri and her four year son Ronnie, along with my wife and two children decided to visit Aunt Francis on Flatbush Ave in Brooklyn. When we arrived at Aunt Francis home, we were greeted with a lot of hugs and kisses. She made you feel very welcome at her home. So we all went into her living room. There they all talked about the old days involving Pat's family. Aunt Frances was the sister of Pat's mom. So they also talked about their experiences growing up. It was nice to see them all laugh about the things that took place during their life. Aunt Frances requested that we all go into the dinning room for lunch. Without any hesitation, we proceeded to the dinning room for a great lunch. After lunch we proceeded back to the living room for more conversation. After we were there for a while, we all agreed it was time to leave for home. Aunt Frances wanted us to take some of her candy that was in the living room for snacks on the way home. There were some Jaw Breakers in a jar, on an end table. We did not take any because they were too hard to eat. We did take some cookies, so the children would have some snacks for our trip back home. So we all gathered up what belongings we had and started walking towards the front door. We weren't aware that little Ronnie had taken some jaw breakers candy and placed some in his pants pocket. He was behind his mother when leaving the living room.

As Helen, Aunt Frances, our children Antoinette and Christopher and Pat and I were near the front door we heard a loud scream. The scream came from Geri while she was still in the living room with Ronnie. We all quickly ran to the living room to see what was going on. Geri was in a panic state, screaming that little Ronnie had swallowed a Jaw Breaker and can't breathe. I observed little Ronnie was choking and turning blue in the face.

I immediately grabbed Ronnie in my arms and turn him up side down and slapped my hands on Ronnie's back. Within seconds a Jaw breaker came out of little Ronnie's mouth. He started to get his normal color back. Every body was so pleased to know I was there to take action to save Ronnie. Geri was so appreciative, she just hugged me. I said thank God that Ronnie is still here. After every one calmed down we went on our way home. Ronnie as of this year 2009 is married and has two children. We had never forgotten that summer day in Flatbush, Brooklyn.

This was truly "God's Work".

Event #7

EVENT #7

Throughout my Law Enforcement career, I was involved with many types of events. It is kind of hard to recall the exact times and dates of all that took place, through out the years. But I do recall the events that did take place. Here is an event that will give you the reader an understanding of "God's Work". It was some time in the mid 1970's; I was a Patrolman for the Rapid City Police Department. As a Patrolman, my duties at the time was to handle calls for service, watch out for speeders, drunken drivers, vehicle accidents, assaults, burglaries, fights and many other public relations activities. The main duties are to protect and serve the people in the community I work at. While I was on patrol in my unit in the area assigned, I received a call in reference to an accident with injuries on East St. Joseph Street, near the School of Mines School. I immediately turned on my emergency lights and siren to my patrol car and headed to the scene of the accident. This is mostly done to get to the scene as quickly as possible without getting any other person hurt on the road. People are to pull over to the side of the road when an emergency vehicle is coming by.

Upon my arrival at the scene, I observed several people looking on. Some of them were yelling out to me there is a person in the vehicle. You see the vehicle was also on fire which made things more dangerous for any rescue to be made. I ran over to the vehicle and observed a young man hurt in the vehicle. He could not move from the vehicle. While the vehicle was still on fire I reached in to pull the victim out of the vehicle. My concern at the time was not his injuries but to get him out of the vehicle to live. As I was pulling the victim out of the vehicle, the Rapid City Fire department arrived. Understand this was taken place in just minutes of the call for the accident. As I pulled the victim out of the vehicle, the Fire Department personnel helped me carry the teenage victim away from the flaming vehicle. Other police units arrived to help with traffic and to keep people from getting too close to the scene. The Ambulance arrived for medical assistance for the victim. I helped the Ambulance Crew place the victim into the ambulance while he was on a stretcher. You can hear the young man calling out to me, as the ambulance was preparing to leave, "Thank You Officer", "Thank

You". I was so please to know the victim did not die at the scene. I did not receive any injuries that would need some medical attention. My uniform obtained some smoke fumes on it. The victim was transported to the Rapid City Regional Hospital.

I had always carried a very small book of prayers in my uniform pocket. No one knew except my wife, that I would say a prayer to get me through my day while working as a police officer. The book is called "A Catholic Book of Prayers" is still in my possession at my home. The prayer to Saint Michael was my favorite. He is the Saint that represents all the Police and Firemen in this country.

The last time I ever heard from the victim, was through my brother Libby. It was sometime in the year 1999 my brother had told me he saw the victim. The victim had moved to Hawaii and was so grateful I had saved his life from the burning vehicle. I had never got to see him at that time. But felt so pleased to hear he is living a normal Life.

This was truly "God's Work".

Event #8

EVENT #8

As I continued with my career in Law Enforcement, the events would continue to add up. I can recall some of the events involved child birth. This event to be told is one of God's greatest miracles. It was a time when I was on patrol, assigned to the Southside of Rapid City called Robbinsdale. As I was traveling south on Elm street from East St. Patrick street, the dispatcher advised me an ambulance is dispatched to a house on Wisconsin Street. I proceeded to the house on Wisconsin Street. When I arrived at the house, an excited man came running to me and said she is inside the house. As we entered the house, I asked him, what's going on? He said his wife is having a baby. He pointed towards the bathroom located off the hall way. I entered the bathroom and there was his wife standing over the toilet bowl. She was giving birth to a baby, while standing up. I asked her to lay down on the floor, so I could help her with the delivery. While she was on the floor I could see the baby was crowning. The baby boy was being born in my hands as a new life begins.

Her husband was at a state of panic and I told him to go outside and direct the ambulance crew to our location. I kept the mother and child in a safe position, on the floor. There in my arms with the cord still attached to the mother, was a God giving gift of life. The ambulance crew arrived and was escorted to our location. One of the crew members asked me if every thing is alright. I observed the husband looked a little pale in the face. I told the ambulance personnel to check the husband out. As an EMT, it was nice to help with the procedure of cutting the baby's cord. It was nice to have been trained as an EMT, to take proper action with helping the mother and baby. The mother was so pleased to have received my help. It was a beautiful site to see both mother and child together on the stretcher. The ambulance took the mother and baby to the Rapid City Regional Hospital for a check up. The husband thanked me for my help, and went off to the hospital.

After the call for service, I headed back to my patrol unit. My call to the Dispatcher was a happy moment for me. My call could be heard by all the units on duty. I said, "it is a healthy baby boy"! The dispatcher on duty responded by saying, "congratulations"! So I went back to my other patrol duties.

You see I had participated in many situations as described above, as an Officer. There are times like this event that makes it all worthwhile.

This was truly "God's Work".

KNIGHTS OF COLUMBUS COUNCIL 1489
MEMORIAL FOR THE UNBORN PROJECT
MAY 21, 2000

Left to Right: Deacon Luis Usera Sr., Bill Spratte, Terry Williams, Francis Paulin, Fr. Dave Orians,
Grand Knight, Abraham Usera, Herm Schneider, Libby Usera, Fred Berensde,
Deacon George Gladfelter, Ernie Garcia, Del Solano, Kevin Rohbach, Bishop Blasé J. Cupich,
John Janssen, Fr. Brian Christensen, Tom Bommershach, Jerry Loomer, Ralph Schwab,
James Washabaught, Msgr. Michael Woster, David Rodarte

Prescribed on the Monument: "WE MUST CHERISH AND PRESERVE THE WORK OF GOD'S HANDS"

Event #9

EVENT #9

It was a beautiful summer day in the year of 1973, in the Black Hills of South Dakota. My wife Pat and I decided to take our two children to the Sheridan Lake area for the day. Sheridan Lake is an area where you can go swimming, fishing, camping and have a nice picnic. We decided to invite our friends to accompany us to the lake. So we gathered up our coolers containing food and drinks. Also our fishing gear, folding chairs, blankets, towels and anything else that was needed for the trip.

So we headed out in our vehicles to travel on Sheridan Lake road to get to the lake. While on the way we observed some deer on the hill side from the road. The deer were just grazing in the field. It was like a picture on the wall. We finely arrived near Sheridan Lake and turned off at a side road. The side road led us to a picnic area approximately fifty feet from the lake. We observed other people in the area, as we looked for a picnic spot for our families. We found a great spot not too far from the lake and settled down there.

After getting settled down, my friend Don and I, along with our children proceeded to go to the lake. Our wives stayed at the picnic area to have time together without the kids around. We took our fishing gears to do a little fishing at the lake. The walk to the lake was a good hike for us all. There was a little hill to walk down to reach the lake. We found a nice flat area next to the lake. The water was so calm and clear, you could see the bottom of the lake. It was also clear enough to see the fish swimming.

Our children were having fun trying to catch the big one. Actually any fish size would have been a great time for them.

As we were fishing, I observed two small children walking towards our direction. They appeared to be approximately two and four years old. They were right of us, approximately fifteen feet from where we were fishing. As I looked over to my left where Don and our children were at; I heard a loud splash on my right. I turned to my right and only observed the four year old standing there looking into the water. When I did not see the two year old I immediately looked into the lake water.

There I could see an image of a child or baby doll. The figure was sinking face down, approximately six feet under the water. With my full clothes on, I immediately dove into the cold lake water. I grabbed the arm of the baby and swam to the shore of the lake.

When I got the child out of the water, he appeared to look blue in the face. I could not feel any breath of air coming from his mouth. I immediately proceeded to do Artificial Respiration. Within seconds I got the child to throw up some water and start to breathe. Thank God life came back to the child. The child also started to cry for his mother. There were no parents near by for the little children. The other little boy pointed to the area where their parents were at. So Don and I along with our children headed back to the picnic area with the two little children. I carried the little boy in my arms to the picnic site where his parents were at. When we got to the top of the hill from the lake, the four year old pointed to the picnic site where their parents were at. We took the small children to their parents. I told them what had taken place involving their children. Their mother was upset that her kids walk away from their picnic site. She grabbed her little boy and said with tears in her eyes," Oh God I could have lost you". It was kind of hard for me not to say anything, but I did. I told the two little boys parents they should have had better eyes on their kid's whereabouts. I also told them to seek medical attention to see if the child is still alright. The parents said they will do that when they leave for home.

Deep in my heart I was still concern for the children. There were no phones in the picnic area and I did not see any Park Rangers. So I hoped the parents were going to do the right thing when they got home. So Don, our children and I proceeded to our picnic site where we advised our wives of the event that took place.

This was truly "God's Work".

Event #10

EVENT #10

During the years of 1978 to 1984 I was assigned to the Criminal Investigation Division for the Rapid City Police Department. The Division was also called the Detectives Division. I served as a Detective and School Liaison Officer for the Division. My assignments consisted of investigating criminal activities, with approximately 30 cases a month. My other duties consisted as a School Liaison Officer involved working with the Rapid City School system. I would handle the West Jr. High, South Jr. High, Central High, Stevens High and all of the grade schools in the South and West sides of Rapid City.

When working at the schools I would be involved with crime prevention and apprehension of Law Violators. There were many times I would also do counseling with the students. I had developed a good relation with the teachers and students. The students had also developed their trust in me for a lot of situations. I would be in plain clothes most of the time I was assigned to duty. I would also wear a uniform during special school sporting events at the Rapid City Civic Center.

What also helped me a lot was my experience with kids and my tactics and specialized training in many fields involving them, for example, attending the Juvenile Officers Institute at the University of Minnesota, Drug Administration Course of instruction with the D.E.A., Drug and Alcohol prevention programs, Training instruction Sexual Assault and Child Molestation with the Forensic Mental Health Association in Rapid City. Sexual Assault and Touch conference on Prevention of Sexual Abuse with the Black Hills State University, Child Abuse, Neglect and Sexual Abuse with the University of South Dakota, Reid Interview and Interrogation School, promoted by the Criminal Investigation Division, Pierre, South Dakota. One that was associated with the following event is the Hostage Negotiation Course with the U.S. Department of Justice Federal Bureau of Investigation.

This event started when I was on duty at one of the assigned schools. A phone call came to me from a concern parent of a High School student. Because of my trust and sincerity I would get calls from students and parents when they felt they needed my help or advice. The mother was a little excited about her 17 year old son. She said, Mr. Usera, I need your help, my son told me he was going to kill himself. I immediately advised her in a calm voice, to try to calm down. I told her I will be en route to her house as soon as possible. When I arrived at the resident, I was immediately approached by the boy's mother at the door. My first concern was to know if any weapons are involved and the location of the Boy and his status at the time. The mother advised me her son has a High Power Rifle in his room, threatening to commit suicide. She also advised me his girlfriend had left him for another boy. I also wanted to know if he was drinking any Alcohol. She didn't feel he would have any alcohol, because he doesn't drink. It was then I told the mother to stay back out of the way as I enter the boy's room.

As I slowly started to enter the boy's room, he looked over towards my direction. He knew me by saying, "Hi Mr. Usera"! I said Hi, back in a gentle voice. There in his hands was a rifle lodge under his throat. I spent some time to clam him down. He explain to me why he so upset about his girl friend leaving him for another boy. It was the time my trust was desperately needed. I was able to get him to take the rifle from his throat. I did everything human to convince him that his life was more important then losing a girlfriend. We talked about all of the good things to look forward to as he grew up to be a man. A simple statement made to him was, "there are many other Fish in the Sea". I finely got the boy to turn over the rifle to me. I asked his mother to come into the room to show him how much she loved him. The boy's father arrived and the rifle was turned over to the father for safe keeping. There were many hugs from the boy to his parents and hugs to me from all present. My advice to the parents was to have their son follow up with some professional counseling. They all thank me and I left the house.

As of this year 2009, the boy is now a grown man with a family. When some of my fellow officers heard about my handling of the event, they thought I was risking my life without any help. My thought at the time was to save a young man from dying.

It was not my intention to be a hero but to do my duties as a professional and to be a caring person. My trust in God helped me to get through this serious situation.

No matter what, it was "God's Work" that got me through this all.

Event #11

EVENT #11

It was a very cold day in November of 1985. I was sitting at my desk as the new Chief of Police for the City of Box Elder, South Dakota. The City of Box Elder had hired me approximately four months prior to November.

As the new Chief of Police and the Public Safety Officer, I had a lot of responsibilities. Some consist of maintaining good public employee and official relations. Make plans, develop procedures, organize and reorganize. Establishing policies and provide direction for the department. The responsibilities I had, never end as Chief of Police. One of the first thing done as Chief of Police was implementing a new dress code. The dress code which also involved me consisted of wearing a sport jacket with a tie or suit or uniform to court. The past Chief of Police did not have a dress code. It was my way of making the department a professional agency.

On that day I was sitting at my desk when a call for help came from the dispatcher. The dispatcher advised me a man was buried in dirt at a closed Gas Station in Box Elder. So I got into my Police Unit and proceeded to the scene. The Gas Station was located near the Ellsworth Air Force Base main gate road.

When I arrived at the scene, there were people pointing to me where the man was buried at. It appeared the man buried was installing a chain over the end of a large underground gasoline tank to remove from the ground. I did not see any part of the man's body but just dirt. I immediately jumped into the dirt pile where the man was possibly buried. I observed a water hose near the closed gas station. A city worker name McKay was near by and I advise him to get the hose. When he brought the hose over to me I cut it a little shorter. Not concern about my new uniform or what could happen to me at the time, I started digging in the area where the man was buried. I finely got to his head. McKay jumped into the area and also started helping me to dig out more dirt. I placed the water hose to the mouth of the victim and continue to dig out more dirt. The dirt that was in the area we were working at, was very cold.

As we were approaching the man's shoulder by digging out more dirt, the Pennington County Search and Rescue Team arrived. Other Law Enforcement personnel arrived to assist with traffic and to help keep people not involved with the rescue out of the danger area. As McKay and I climbed out of the whole we were full of dirt all over our clothes. My new uniform looked like it had been around for many years. Some of the people in the area started clapping their hands for our rescue work. It was a proud moment for McKay and me. No matter what, it was my duty to do the right thing at the time. A man's life was in danger and we had to act. As the Team took over the rest of the rescue, an Ellsworth Air Force Base Ambulance arrived to administered oxygen to the victim while being help out of the hole. Boards were propped against the edges so the dirt wouldn't fall back into the area where the rescue was taken place. After a great effort by all involved the man was finely pulled out of the hole. The Ellsworth Air Force Base Ambulance then transported the victim to the Rapid City Regional Hospital. The victim was treated and released from the Hospital.

On December 13, 1985, the Rapid City Journal news paper article read, The Governor of South Dakota, William Janklow presented certificates of Life Saving to Chief of Police Abraham Usera and City worker Craig McKay for the November 1985 Rescue.

As I had always said, I just did what my God wanted me to do, and that is to help those in need. It is so nice to know the victim was given a second chance in life.

This was truly "God's Work".

**Box Elder City, South Dakota,
Chief of Police Abraham Usera and wife Patricia,
at the 1987 Police Reserves Graduation Ceremony.**

It was the first time the Box Elder City Police department ever held the training for Reserve Officers in Box Elder City. Seven new Reserve Officers Graduated with certification with the Criminal Investigation Division, Law Enforcement Training Center, Pierre, South Dakota.

Abe and Pat's 25th renew of vows at the Cathedral of Our Lady of Perpetual Help Church.

Event #12

EVENT #12

It was a time in my life when things were getting tuff to handle. You see when my son died on July 13, 1987 it was hard for my wife and I to handle the loss. Everything around us, where we lived, had to do with Chris. It was suggested by some that we seek professional help dealing with the lost of our son. After seeking help, we came to the conclusion to leave the area of South Dakota for a change in our lives.

It was the year of 1989 we decided to move to Key West Florida. There my wife was able to continue her work in the Medical field and I in Law Enforcement. She was able to work for the Lower Florida Keys Hospital and I with the Key West Police Department. The move did not take our thoughts and love for Chris away but did give us a chance for some healing. We did not have the continuing questions about his accident and the connection so many people had with him. It kept us from doing our every day living together and the stress placed upon us.

First, a little about Key West, Florida, the year round average temperature was 86 degrees. It is surrounded by the waters of the Atlantic Ocean and the Gulf of Mexico. You are approximately 90 miles from Cuba. It is also an all year round vacation spot for people from all over the world. We attended Saint Mary Star of the Sea Catholic Church. It is the oldest Catholic Parish in South Florida.

The following event took place on a day in August 1989, in Key West, Florida. I was working for the Key West Police Department as a Patrolman. It was the grave yard shift, which consisted of the hours of 11 p.m. to 7 a.m. While on patrol, I received a call from dispatch, a man was attacked by some members of a motorcycle gang. The victim was working as a night janitor at the time. The location was Sloppy Joes on Duval Street. It is one of the most popular places to go in Key West. Upon arrival at the scene, I assisted with the apprehension of the two motor cycle gang members as they attempt to leave the scene. After the apprehension, the suspects were placed into the police wagon and transported to the County Jail for incarceration.

As I looked over to the area of Sloppy Joes, there were many people standing there. As I approached the area I observed a man facing the crowd away from me. I can hear him saying, "Please help me". I did not see any one reaching out to help him. I touched the man on the shoulder and he immediately turn to face me. There I saw a Black Man bleeding profusely from his chest near his heart. He looked into my eyes with his frighten eyes and said to me, "Oh God please don't let me die". I immediately placed my hand on his chest over the area where he was bleeding, with direct pressure. As I was helping him down to the ground to do better direct pressure to the wound, I told him God will help. I yelled over to my fellow officers to get some clean towels. I wanted the towels to help with the first aid for the wound until the Ambulance arrived. It appeared the victim was stabbed with a knife by one of the members of the motor cycle gang. The ambulance arrived and transported the victim to the Lower Florida Keys Hospital for treatment.

The victim had gone through emergency surgery and with the help from the good Doctors, he survived the operation. As he was recovering from his injury he kept asking the hospital personnel to see the Police Officer that saved his life. He described the officer as the one that had dark hair and a dark mustache that looked like a Mexican. One of the medical personnel present at the time was my wife. She told him she thinks she knows who the Police Officer was. When my wife told me about the request of the victim, I went to the Hospital to visit him. As I entered the Intensive Care Unit, the victim immediately removed his oxygen mask from his face. He started crying and asked me to come closer to him. He than grabbed me and hugged me tightly. He just kept saying, "No one would help me or even touch me", but you. "You saved my life". It was kind of hard not to have tears in my eyes for the victim. I just told him, "thank God for his help", and I was happy everything turned out okay for him.

I always wondered why no one had helped him. Was it because of his race or did they think he had Aids, or maybe because it was the Deep South. We will never have the answer, but do thank God things turned out in favor for the victim.

On August 28, 1989 the Key West Police Department presented me a Certificate of Commendation for the life saving of the victim, by the Chief of Police, Webster and Supervisor Lieutenant Bethel.

As I continue to state, it was "God's Work".

Abe Usera as a Police Officer
For the
Key West Police Department in Fl.

Conclusion
of
Events

CONCLUSION OF EVENTS

I have talked about events involving some of my family members.

They consisted of my brothers and sister and nephew.

The next few events consist of my immediate family.

They would be my Wife, Daughter and Son.

The following events involved their heartfelt fight for life, accomplishments and their love for our Lord our God.

Event #13

EVENT #13

This event involves Christopher Abraham Usera, my son, known as Chris. He died in an accident at the age of twenty one, on July 13, 1987, while attempting to help a friend, in New York City.

Through out his short life on earth he was a very active person. Before I get into the event Chris was involved with, here are some of his accomplishments: Member of the school councils from the fourth to the eight grade played Viola in Grade School and Junior High School Orchestras. He also played Drums with the Band and Orchestra at Central High School. The schools are all located in Rapid City, South Dakota. He had received numerous recognitions for achievements for many activities he was involved with. Some include being a member of the Central High School Debate Team. He was chosen all City Debater in 1982. He was elected to be a member of The National Forensic League, a degree of honor. Chris served as an Altar Boy at the Cathedral of Our Lady of Perpetual Help. He played on teams involving many sports activities. He was a member of the Knights of Columbus Council 1489, Boy Scout Troop 7. As a Scout he earned the religious Ad Altare Dei medal. In the year 1980, he received the medal during a Mass at the Cathedral. Chris became an Eagle Scout in May of 1980. He was also a member of the Rapid City Police Department Explorer Post 110 Police Cadets and also served in the United States Air Force. There were many other activities that took place during his life, and I feel you have some idea of what kind of person Chris was.

In relation to this event, Christopher as a member of Boy Scout Troop 7 worked hard to reach his goal in becoming an Eagle Scout. There were several Merit Badges required for him to become an Eagle Scout. One of them was the First Aid Merit Badge. As the instructor for the First Aid Merit Badge, the boys in the troop, including Chris, had to take written and physical test to earn their merit badges.

The event took place on a cold and winter day of January 7, 1979, in Rapid City. There were many children out and about playing in the snow. They would build snow men, snow ball fighting and sledding down hills. Chris and his friend Richard went to the corner of Oak and Indiana Streets for sledding. There was a large hill where many children, including adults would go sledding on sleds and inner tubes. There at the top of the hill stood two young men approximately 28 years old. They were preparing to get on an inner tube, after the children in front of them went first. So the men got onto their inner tube and proceeded down the hill. The inner tube they were on traveled very fast going down hill. The hill was very steep, which caused everyone to travel fast down the hill. The heavy the person, the faster the ride would be. As the two men were heading down the hill, the inner tube they were on started to head in another direction from the path. When they hit bottom they rammed into a large utility pole. One of the men, age 28, was in very bad pain.

At the top of the hill was twelve year old, Boy Scout, First Class Chris. He observed the accident and quickly jumped on his sled with his friend, and proceeded down hill to the accident scene. When Chris arrived at the scene he could see the man was in serious pain. Chris immediately placed his coat over the victim in freezing temperature. He also advised the bystanders at the scene not to move the man. So Chris ran to the nearest house to summon an Ambulance. The Ambulance arrived and transported the injured man to the Rapid City Regional Hospital for treatment. The man was treated and released from the hospital. The result of the man's injury was that he suffered five fractured ribs. Because of Christopher's coolness and leadership averted a worse situation and reflected much credit upon him and his scout training, received the Medal of Merit for Meritorious Action, from the National Boys Scouts of America office.

His willingness to help those in need of help is a reflection on his parents.

This was truly "God's Work".

"God Bless Christopher "

**Christopher age 10, serving as an Altar Boy with
Bishop Lawrence Harold Welsh,
at the
Cathedral of Our Lady of Perpetual Help
(October 1976)**

**The presentation of the Boy Scouts of America,
Religious Ad Altare Dei Medal
Rev. Michel Mulloy presented the Catholic Boy Scout
Medal to Christopher Abraham Usera
with his parents present, at the
Cathedral of Our Lady of Perpetual Help Church, in 1980**

The Boy Scouts of America presents different kinds of medals to represent all of the religious faith that believe in God to the Boy Scouts that earn them.

Event #14

EVENT #14

Having a family is one of the best gifts God has ever given me. For me, personally having children is a great adventure in life and watching the smiles when they are happy and the tears when they are sad. To know they are full of love and happiness when they see their parents at their school and sporting events.

As for my daughter Antoinette known as Toni, was full of energy for the things she loved. When she was a child, she would always sing and dance to all kinds of music. As she entered grade school she immediately got into the grove of music. When she was in her kindergarten class she was classified as Miss Alphabet, because she was the lead singer in her class. Actually she was the lead singer through out her school years. Toni was in the Girl Scouts and also participated in Little League Softball. As parents we were proud of her achievements with the activities she was involved with. She sang at her High School graduation. She was also a member of the All State Choir, for the state of South Dakota. At the Loyal Day Parade, she participated in the Queen contest. She sang up a storm for the people present and was chosen the Loyal Day Queen, which was sponsored by Rapid City V.F.W. She later got married at the Cathedral of Our Lady of Perpetual Help, and started to have a family. Her first child was name Jesse.

An event that took place in her life was when she was working at the Prairie Bottle Store on East New York Street, in Rapid City. She was a cashier at the time. A male subject walked into the store started looking around. Toni at the time was eight months pregnant with her second child. Jesse was three years old, at home with his dad. The man waited till the other customers left the store, leaving just Toni and him. The man pulled a hand gun out of his pocket and put it at Toni's face. He demanded money from the cash register. As a Law Enforcement Officer I had always told my family and others, not to resist. Just give the suspects the money. My daughter did what the suspect wanted. As she was reaching for the money she thought it would be a good idea to lean her Pregnant Belly on the silent alarm button on the counter. The suspect did not hear any alarm and continued with the holdup.

Thank God he did not hurt Toni and left the store. When the suspect went out to the parking lot of the store, he was met by Rapid City Finest, the Rapid City Police Department. The suspect was apprehended with the help of my dear daughter Toni. I went with my daughter to the trial for support. The result of the trial, the suspect was sentence to prison for the Arm Robbery.

Toni had experience some sad times in her life. She had lost her brother and had a divorce. She had throughout her life raised four boys without any father for her sons. As parents and grandparents we were there to help as much as we could. She kind of kept away from the church until later in her life. She still had that love for singing and she got into the spirit. She went to St. Isaac Jogues Church where she joined the choir. That's when God's Work took place. She sang so well the people that attend St Isaac would attend more often just to hear her sing.

As most people would say, she has a voice of an Angel. They heard her sing at church and at funerals. She is also involved with many church functions, such as the Flowers of Many Colors. Help with feeding the poor each month. My wife and I always felt she would get back to her faith again. Toni continues her singing for the Church and for God Almighty.

Her two oldest boys, Jesse had graduated from the Black Hills State University, in South Dakota and Keith at the University of Minnesota. The other two boys, Alan and Jeremy are in High School. All of the boys had gone through the Sacraments of the Church.

The result is reflected in "God's Work".

Some of the Sacraments of the Catholic Church
Involving our daughter Antoinette

At Baptism with Abe and Pat Usera in 1964, at the St. Elizabeth Church
In Ozone Park, Queens, New York.

At First Holy Communion, in 1972, at the Our Lady of Perpetual Help Church
In Rapid City, South Dakota.

Event #15

EVENT #15

This event takes place close to home. The person involved is a Mother, Grandmother, Best Friend, Sister, Coach, Leader, a believer of our Lord Jesus Christ. She is my wife Patricia, known as Pat. She was born to her parents, Frank and Helen Bile'. She has two sisters, Virginia (Gin) and Geraldine (Geri) and one brother, Stephen (Steve). She was also an Associate Advisor for the Rapid City Police Cadets Explorer Post110. And a Committee Member for the Knights of Columbus Council 1489, Boy Scout Troop 7. After 28 years, she has retired from working in the Medical Profession. She has gone through a lot of good times and sad ones in her life. A couple of real sad times in her life involved the lost of her baby boy at birth. Another one involves the lost of another son, Christopher age twenty One. No matter where we lived she never complained about anything that has taken place. To me she is one of a kind. She always makes time to say a rosary each day.

This event first takes place in the year 1993. We were living in Key West Florida. When we moved to Key West we always made trips back to Rapid City, South Dakota to visit our family. The way we traveled there was by Car. A round trip was approximately 5,000 miles. In the summer time of 1993, we visit our daughter, grandchildren and other family members. When we were at our daughters' house we help with some painting. Pat felt some thing was not right with her. When she was helping redecorate she felt an uncomfortable pressure in her chest. Thinking it was nothing at the time she continued to do other things. We later went with some family members to a restaurant. While there Pat mentioned to me she was having the same symptoms. It was our intention to leave the next morning for our trip back home to Key West.

So we made the decision to go to the Rapid City Regional Hospital for a check up for Pat. The doctor in the emergency room told Pat to seek more test when she returns home to Key West. I knew that some other test should be done at the hospital before we left for the trip. Because it was a very long trip on the road, I was very concerned. So I asked the doctor, if my wife was his sister or wife would he recommend Pat should stay over night for more test. At that time, the doctor agreed, due to family history, Pat should stay over night for more tests. So Pat agreed to stay over to make sure she was alright for the trip. While Pat was at the hospital, I stayed over at my mother's house, because she lived close to the hospital.

At approximately 5:30 a.m. in the morning, it happened. Pat was having a heart attack. The hospital personnel was trying to locate me, but was unsuccessful because I was on my way to the hospital at the time. The hospital staff took Pat into the surgery room. There the procedure called Angioplasty was done on Pat. There were some blocked arteries found in Pat. We truly believe God was with Pat during her ordeal, which could get worse. After treatment she was released from the hospital. Thank God we did not get on the road without a stay over. I thanked the Doctors for their decision to follow up on Pat's condition.

Throughout the years followed, Pat had taken yearly stress test for her heart. She kept up with a strict food diet and did not smoke or use alcohol. Her heart problem is considered hereditary, which was related to her mother and fathers heart problems. It was mentioned to Pat through out the years her stress test results showed she was doing fine.

It was in the year 2008 when she was up for her yearly stress test, when this next event involving Pat took place. Pat was told her stress test results were fine. But Pat felt the symptoms she was having made her feel the stress test is not telling the truth. She advised me she feels some pressure on her chest and some pain down her left arm. It was that time of the year we had planned to meet her two sisters and brother for a family reunion. This was going to take place at her brother's home in Michigan. After the reunion we plan on traveling to New York City to go to a New York Yankee game. It was going to be the last year the Yankees were going to play at the old stadium. You can see we are true Yankee fans. The new stadium was to open in 2009.

So Pat and I made a decision to find another doctor for a second opinion before we took our trip. So we finely found another heart doctor for a second opinion. It was like de ja vu in reference to the year 1993. We met with the new doctor and he said the stress test shows the results are fine for Pat. So I recommended to the Doctor, due to Pats complaint about her arm and chest, to have more test to be done. I mentioned to him a catheterization should be done on Pat. The doctor agreed with me and ordered a Cardio Catheterization, because it has been awhile since her last one. I asked the doctor if everything goes well for Pat, when we can get on the road to travel. He said the next day.

So Pat and I proceeded to the Rapid City Regional Hospital for the scheduled procedure. As I sat in the waiting room, the doctor came out of the surgery room and advised me of the result of the exam. He said Pat has four blocked areas of her arteries to her heart. There was also an Aneurysm in one of the arteries. Three Stents were placed in to her arteries and the Aneurysm was also removed.

You see Pat could have been in trouble if she went on the trip without the exam. We did not take the trip after the procedure, due to Pats rehab care.

Telling the story of Pats events hopefully will help those that might have similar symptoms. We again thank the doctor for his understanding to do the right thing. I thank my dear wife for her willingness to allow me to tell her story. I specially thank God for giving Pat a second chance of life.

This was truly "God's Work ".

"God's Work"
Charity

Pat Usera helping serving people at the Knights of Columbus Council 1489 booth. The booth is part of a fund raising drive the council does every year at the Pennington County State Fair in Rapid City, South Dakota.

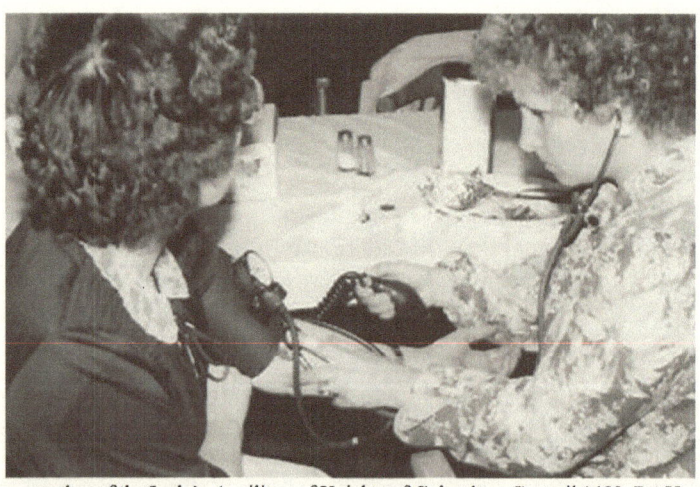

As a member of the Lady's Auxiliary of Knights of Columbus Council 1489, Pat Usera helps with the Health Fair project at the Council 1489 Hall. She is taking blood pressure at no charge for the public.

> 1982 Rapid City Police Explorer Post 110
> Graduation Ceremony held at the Rapid City Civic Center.

> Cadet Advisor Senior Officer Abe Usera with Guest Speaker
> South Dakota Lt. Governor Lowell Hansen
> and Associate Advisor Pat Usera

ENDING OF THE EVENTS:

I hope you the reader had enjoyed the events told in this book.

As told in the beginning, the events were all true.

It's my hope the events told will help those of you to better understand what GOD means to us all.

No matter what faith you believe in, there truly is a GOD. Never give up to the bad things that happen in your life. Just keep on living a good life, by loving and serving GOD.

Especially to remember GOD'S WORK.

THE VOICE OF THE CATHEDRAL

Serving the communities of Rapid City, Hermosa and Keystone

I wish to congratulate one of our parishioners, Abe Usera, Grand Knight for Knights of Columbus Bishop Dimmerling Council #1489, who was just named South Dakota JFK Knights of Columbus Knight of the Year 2000. Abe was selected out of the 8000 members of the Knights in South Dakota for his 28 years continued service to our church and community. This honor highlights Abe's service in the Knights and their many generous projects and also in the Boy Scouts. He has guided 19 young men into the Eagle Scout level. His Council also brought home awards for Youth Activity, Council Activity and Elite, and first place award in membership development out of 100 councils. Our parish is fortunate and blessed to have such generous and dedicated men so focused on giving back to the Lord for the many blessing in their lives. As Pastor, I would like to thank you for your strong support and service to our parish needs. Congratulations, Abe!

In Christ's Peace,

Msgr. Michael Woster

Council 1489 hosts 1017 people at Thanksgiving feed

THANKSGIVING FEED--Council 1489 held its annual Thanksgiving feed. Some of the 1017 people had a free meal Thanksgiving Day. Approximately 130 individuals volunteered their time. Almost 500 individuals take in the feed in years past, but 1999 was double the average in attendance.

Photo from The Crusader dated January 2000

PREPARING TURKEY—Some of the Council 1489 members prepare the 39 turkeys for the Thanksgiving feed. Members include from left, Ernie Garcia, Herm Schneider, Buck Healey and Grand Knight Abe Usera.

THE KNIGHTS OF COLUMBUS COUNCIL 1489 TOY DRIVE—1999
"GOD'S WORK" -
GIVING TO THE NEEDED

Grand Knight Abe Usera with some of the toys collected for the children at Saint Frances'
Mission on the Pine Ridge Indian Reservation.

Right to Left: Brother Knight Libby Usera, Santa Claus and Grand Knight Abe Usera.
The truck was donated by Rapid City Servall Linen Company to deliver the hundreds of
toys to the Saint Frances' Mission in South Dakota.

**Abe and Pat Usera at prayer near the Altar of the
St. Ambrose Church in Deadwood South Dakota
(Christmas Mass of 2008)**

ABE'S FAMILY AS OF THIS
DATE AND TIME 2010

Sister:

Carmen is married to Tom, with five children and also with grandchildren. Carmen is a manager for a department store. Tom had Served in the U.S. Army and is a Police Officer for a University in South Dakota.

Brothers:

John is a Ph.D., and is married to Bernadette, with three children, and they also have grandchildren. John had served with the U.S. Marines and is a member of the Knights of Columbus. He is a President and CEO for a Foundation.

Luis Sr. is married to Teresa, and they had seven children. Four had gone to Heaven. They also have grandchildren. He also adopted three girls. Luis is retired from the U.S. Air Force as a Master Sergeant. He has been a Catholic Deacon for over 25 years. He is a member of the Knights of Columbus. Both Luis and Teresa had been chosen as the State of South Dakota Knights of Columbus Family of the year 2005.

Roland has two children and also grandchildren. He had served with the U.S. Army. He is now retired as a Civil Service Employee.

Libby is married to Valerie with three children and grandchildren. He had served in the U.S. Army. He is a Manager for Linen Company. He is also a member of the Knights of Columbus.

Carlos is married to Maria. They have four children and also grandchildren. Carlos is a retired Major from the U.S. Army. He is a Director in a Civil Service Position. He is also a member of the Knights of Columbus.

Julio known as Mutch, is married to Char, with four children and grandchildren. Mutch is a Director for an Electricity and Power Corporation.

Mario is married to Cari, with one child. He is a President of a Bank.

Isaac has three children. He is a construction worker.

The following pages consist of Abe's Community Volunteer Work and Recognitions bestowed to Abe as a Law Enforcement Officer and Community Volunteer:

COMMUNITY INVOLVEMENT—

AN APPRECIATION FOR OUR BISHOP'S SUPPORT FOR THE KNIGHTS OF COLUMBUS COUNCIL 1489

At the Bishop's Monthly Luncheon, which was held at the Knights of Columbus Council 1489 Hall, Grand Knight Abe Usera presented to Bishop Blase J. Cupich A Knights of Columbus Jacket, on February 4, 2000

Little League Manager for Softball and Baseball- Harney Little League, Rapid City South Dakota.

Internal Director for the Rapid City Jaycees.

Youth Chairman for the Knights of Columbus Council 1489, Rapid City.

Member of the West River Alcohol Advisory Board, Rapid City.

Chairman for the United Way, Rapid City.

Scout Master for Boy Scout Troop 7, Rapid City. During that time Abe help produce 19 Eagle Scouts.

Advisor for the Rapid City Police Department, Explorer Post 110, Police cadets.

C.P.R. Instructor for the American Red Cross in Rapid City.

Multi-Media, and Advance First Aid Instructor for the American Red Cross in Rapid City.

Member of the Indian and White Relations Committee.

Member of the Rapid City Child Abuse Team.

Member of the Alcohol/Drug Abuse Team, Pennington County, South Dakota.

Member of the Cathedral of Perpetual Help Church, Fall Festival Committee in Rapid City.

Member of the Muscular Dystrophy Association, for South Dakota.

Involved with the Special Olympics, (United States).

Board member of the International Sports Corporation in Rapid City.

Board Member of the Rapid City Police Association.

Played Santa Claus for the Rapid City St Johns Hospital Children's Ward.

Child Safety and Rape Prevention Lectures for the Rapid City YMCA.

Helped with the Rapid City Clean-Up for several years.

Helped with the March of Dimes Charity work with the Ellsworth Air Force Base Personnel.

Chairman for the Cystic Fibrosis Foundation in Box Elder City, South Dakota.

Chairperson for the Box Elder City Equal Employment Opportunity Commission.

Participated in the Special Olympics Torch Runs in Spearfish, South Dakota (1987) And Key West, Florida (1989) and (1990).

Held Positions with the Knights of Columbus Council 1489, Rapid City as the Grand Knight, Deputy Grand Knight, Trustee, Youth Chairman and led in many activities involving Church, Charity and Community Work with the council.

Spent many hours with Crime Prevention Programs while off duty as a Law Enforcement Officer. Programs consist of Child Abuse, Alcohol and Drug Abuse, Rape Prevention, Home and Business Protection.

Some of the Recognitions Abe received as a Dedicated Law Enforcement Officer and as a Citizen in the Communities he lived in.

Letter of Commendation from Rapid City, South Dakota Mayor Art LaCroix.

Citation for outstanding service and exemplary conduct during the performance of his duties as a Law Enforcement Officer for the City of Rapid City, from Chief of Police Ronald Messer.

Seven Letters of Commendations presented by Rapid City Chief of Police Jim Anderson and Chief of Police Ray Neal.

A Letter of Commendation from Sturgis, South Dakota Chief of Police Russell B. Hilton.

Two Letters of Commendation from Key West, Florida Chief of Police Thomas E. Webster.

A Certificate of Commendation for saving a Mans Life from Chief of police Thomas E. Webster. (1989)

Two Letters of Commendation from Rapid City Assistant Chief of Police Stanley B. Zakinski and Assistant Chief of Police Thomas L. Hennies.

Three Letters of Commendation from Rapid City Captains Joe Corneliuson and Captain Thomas L. Hennies.

A Letter of Commendation from South Dakota Attorney General William J. Janklow.

A letter of Commendation from the Chief of Security for the Adjutant Generals Office, State of South Dakota, Robert L. Mayer.

A Letter of Commendation from Rapid City Assistant City Attorney Timothy F. Tobin.

A Letter of Commendation from Chief Assistant State Attorney, Sixteenth Judicial Circuit of Florida, Key West Fl., Jonathan G. Ellsworth.

A Letter of Commendation from the Director of Personnel Actions Department, Air Force Headquarters, Strategic Air Command, Colonel Dillard D. Bolls.

A Letter of Commendation from the Department of the Air Force, Lt. General James P. Mullins.

Officer of the Quarter Award, Rapid City Police Department, Off Duty Volunteer Work From Lt. James Colon (1977)

Citation for Life Saving in 1985, from the Governor of South Dakota William J. Janklow.

Received an Award for Outstanding Service, Dedication and Leadership as Chief of Police for the City of Box Elder from Mayor Sam Boykin and the Police Department personnel. (1987)

First Police Officer in History in the Rapid City area to receive the Outstanding Young Man Award in 1977, from the Rapid City Jaycees.

Outstanding Law Enforcement Award in 1980, from the Rapid City Jaycees.

In 1980 First Police Officer in Rapid City to receive the Saint George Scouting Leadership award presented by Western Catholic Diocese of South Dakota, Bishop Harold Dimmerling.

In 1981 First Police Officer in the Black Hills area Boy Scout Program to receive the District Award of Merit, the highest honor given in a Boy Scout District.

Recipient of the Jaycees Presidential Award of Honor from the Rapid City Jaycees (1980).

Recipient of the Distinguished Service Award from the Veterans of Foreign Wars of the United States in 1983.

Recipient of the KELO-LAND Television Outstanding Public Service to the Community ward, presented by President of the KELO-Land Stations- Evans Nord (1982).

Recipient of the 1988 Governor's Volunteer of the Year Award as a Citationist by South Dakota Governor Mickelson.

Certificate of Achievement in Recognition of Voluntary Service to the Community from Rapid City Mayor Art LaCroix

Recipient of the State of South Dakota Knights of Columbus- Knight of the Year 2000. Presented by Supreme Representative-Judge Richardo Garcia of Texas and South Dakota Deputy Leo Keiser.

As a member of the Knights of Columbus Council 1489, Rapid City, Abe had received the Knight of the Month four times by Grand Knight G. J. O'Neil and Grand Knight Terry Williams.

KOTA Radio 1380 and the Rushmore Mall, Rapid City, S.D., Black Hills Volunteer Salute Certificate for Recognition for the Work Done to Make the Black Hills a Better Place to Live. Presented by Ted Peiffer (KOTA Radio) and Karen Waltman (Rushmore Mall) -2001.

Volunteer Service Award from The Cystic Fibrosis Foundation for recognition and appreciation of volunteer service in the fight to secure a future for those with Cystic Fibrosis and being the Chairman, CF Bowl for Breath, Dakota's Chapter, CFF. 1986.

Award from the United Way Organization, Rapid City, for being the Chairperson of the Week in 1982.

THE FOLLOWING ARE SOME OF THE ORGANIZATIONS THAT PRESENTED ABE WITH LETTERS OF APPRECIATION FOR HIS VOLUNTEER WORK. (CONSIST OF Drug and Alcohol Abuse, Women Safety, Child Abuse, Crime Prevention, Halloween Safety, Career Day, CPR, First Aid Training, Understanding the Laws, and the Police Cadet Program.

South Dakota Women Highway Safety Leaders- Myrnaloy Smith-Dist. VI Director-1980.

Ellsworth Air Force Base, South Dakota, Catholic Youth Program, Elizabeth J. Bowes, Youth Ministry Director-1983

American National Red Cross, Rapid City, Salvatore J. Gentle Executive Director-1980.

Magnetic Peripherals, Inc., Rapid City, R.G. Pickarts, President, M.P.I. Professional Employees Club-1981.

For the work Abe done for the Rapid City Police Cadet Program, South Dakota Lieutenant Governor Lowell C. Hansen, II-1982.

Black Hills Training Center on Drug Abuse, Joyce M. Hulm, Nurse Educator-1984.

West River Alcoholism Services, Rapid City- Staff In service Training in the Course of CPR, Patricia Engebretson, Executive Director-1983.

South Dakota Chapter, Western Division, March of Dimes, and Jail & Bail Fund Drive. Chairperson Mary Linda McBride - 1987.

Carrousel School, Ellsworth Air Force Base, South Dakota, Joan Lankowitz, Principal-1986.

Certificate of Appreciation-Sugarloaf School, Sugarloaf Key, Florida-B. Jobonas-1990

FINAL NOTE

Abe had received many more Awards and Letters of Appreciation for his work.

He was pleased to help those involved with the programs listed.

The work Abe done to help those in need was a life long experience, from his childhood to the present years of his Adult life. He is so pleased to know the results of his work helped many people.

We hope you now can understand what kind of person Abraham "Abe" Usera" is and how he continued to do "GOD'S WORK".

Understanding the work of being a Law Enforcement Officer consisted of possibly being Assaulted while performing his or her duties, receiving Injuries or Death.

Information was obtained from the National Law Enforcement Officer Memorial, Washington D.C.

As of January 2010, approximately 900,000 sworn Law Enforcement Officers now serving in the United States, which is the highest figure ever. About 12 percent of those are Females.

Crime fighting has taken its toll. Since the first recorded Police Death in 1792, there have been more than 18,600 Law Enforcement Officers killed in the line of duty.

A total of 1,640 Law Enforcement Officers died in the line of duty during the past 10 years. An average of one death every 53 hours or 164 per year.

An average of more than 60,000 Law Enforcement Officers are assaulted each year, resulting in approximately 16,000 Injuries.

You know when a Law Enforcement Officer is killed, the Cop Killer will claim more than One Victim, every time.

That's because there's a family of a Law Enforcement Officer in your area, living in fear that today may be the day their loved one does not come home alive! They do have a good reason for that fear, because of the aforementioned information about the Officers killed while on duty. Understand that every day a husband or wife will answer the door and find an Officer there with a grim-face, hat in hand. As their knees buckle, they will not even have to be told what has happened.

Also every day a child will learn that Mommy or Daddy will never be coming Home. And will never again hold them in their arms, and cheer for them at a sporting event. They may never see them graduate or get married. Also a parent will learn that a child they loved so much and are so proud of has been taken away at far too young an age.

Understand that's the message every Law Enforcement Family hopes and pray each and every day they will not receive.

It's Abe's belief that all of his fellow Officers are doing God's Work.

When Abe became a Law Enforcement Officer, he swore under oath to do his duties for his Country and God. He retired from Law Enforcement and had received injuries while performing his duties as a Law Enforcement Officer.

So please keep our Public safety officials, including Law Enforcement Officers, Firefighters, Military, and Emergency workers in your prayers.

They are truly part of "GOD'S WORK"

Abe Usera with his family, Patricia his wife, Christopher and Antoinette
At the
Baltimore City, Maryland Police Academy
Graduation Ceremony (1974)

www.ingramcontent.com/pod-product-compliance
Lightning Source LLC
Chambersburg PA
CBHW030347290526
45785CB00004B/1632